William Kamkwamba
Powering his Village

CORINE
NATIONALE
PREIS
2010

BUCHPREIS
2010

Kylie Burns

Crabtree Publishing Company
www.crabtreebooks.com

Author: Kylie Burns

Series research and development: Reagan Miller

Editorial director: Kathy Middleton

Editor: Crystal Sikkens

Proofreader: Janine Deschenes

Photo researcher: Crystal Sikkens

Designer and prepress technician: Samara Parent

Print coordinator: Katherine Berti

Photographs:
Alamy: ©epa european pressphoto agency b.v.: title page

Getty Images: ©Bobby Longoria: cover, page 29; ©Lucas Oleniuk: page 5, page 14, pages 16-17, page 21; ©Jordan Naylor: page 17 (right); © Ida Mae Astute: pages 24-25

istockphoto: ©Rob Cruse: page 26

Shutterstock.com: ©Brendan Howard: page 6; ©Leonard Zhukovsky: page 22; ©John Wollwerth: page 27

Wikimedia Commons: ©Erik (HASH) Hersman: page 4, page 15 (left), pages 18-19, page 20 (both); ©Stefan Schäfer, Lich: page 19 (right); © Kane5187: page 28; ©Joshdboz: page 30

All other images from Shutterstock

About the author: Kylie Burns is the author of more than a dozen books for children. When she was young, she dreamed of becoming a writer and a teacher. Education helped her achieve those dreams. She hopes William Kamkwamba's story will encourage young people to persevere in every situation so they, too, can realize their dreams.

Library and Archives Canada Cataloguing in Publication

Burns, Kylie, author
   William Kamkwamba : powering his village / Kylie Burns.

(Remarkable lives revealed)
Includes index.
Issued in print and electronic formats.
ISBN 978-0-7787-2690-6 (hardback).--
ISBN 978-0-7787-2701-9 -- (paperback).--ISBN 978-1-4271-1811-0 (html).

   1. Kamkwamba, William, 1987- --Juvenile literature.
2. Mechanical engineers--Malawi--Biography--Juvenile literature.
3. Windmills--Malawi--Juvenile literature. 4. Electric power
production--Malawi--Juvenile literature. 5. Irrigation--Malawi--
Juvenile literature. I. Title.

TJ140 K36 B87 2016   j621.4'53092   C2016-904107-7
                                                C2016-904108-5

Library of Congress Cataloging-in-Publication Data

Names: Burns, Kylie, author.
Title: William Kamkwamba : powering his village / Kylie Burns.
Description: St Catharines, Ontario ; New York, New York : Crabtree
   Publishing Company, [2016] | Series: Remarkable lives revealed |
   Audience: Ages 7-10. | Audience: Grades 4 to 6. | Includes index.
Identifiers: LCCN 2016026657 (print) | LCCN 2016028160 (ebook) |
   ISBN 9780778726906 (reinforced library binding) |
   ISBN 9780778727019 (pbk.) | ISBN 9781427118110 (Electronic HTML)
Subjects: LCSH: Kamkwamba, William, 1987- --Juvenile literature. |
   Mechanical engineers--Malawi--Biography--Juvenile literature. |
   Windmills--Malawi--Juvenile literature. | Electric power
   production--Malawi--Juvenile literature. | Irrigation--Malawi--Juvenile
   literature.
Classification: LCC TJ140.K36 B87 2016 (print) | LCC TJ140.K36 (ebook)
   | DDC 621.4/53092 [B] --dc23
LC record available at https://lccn.loc.gov/2016026657

Crabtree Publishing Company
www.crabtreebooks.com   1-800-387-7650

Printed in Canada/082016/TL20160715

**Published
in Canada
Crabtree Publishing**
616 Welland Ave.
St. Catharines, Ontario
L2M 5V6

**Published in
the United States
Crabtree Publishing**
PMB 59051
350 Fifth Ave., 59th Floor
New York, NY 10118

**Published in the
United Kingdom
Crabtree Publishing**
Maritime House
Basin Road North, Hove
BN41 1WR

**Published
in Australia
Crabtree Publishing**
3 Charles Street
Coburg North
VIC, 3058

Contents

Power and Hope

Every person has a unique story to tell. Stories about remarkable people are sometimes told and remembered by many people, while others aren't as widely known. We all have different ideas about what makes someone remarkable. Creativity and hope are two remarkable qualities that William Kamkwamba (kam-kuh-WOM-buh) showed when he was forced to leave school and help his parents by working. Even though he was no longer able to attend school, William was determined to continue learning and made remarkable things happen. His accomplishments inspire people all over the world.

What is a Biography?

A biography is the story of a person's experiences. We read biographies to learn more about a person's life. A biography is based on primary sources, such as a person's own words or pictures, and secondary sources such as information from friends, family, media, and research.

William Kamkwamba built his community's first windmill.

Remarkable William

After reading a book about the power of the wind, William decided to make a windmill. He created an "electric wind" machine for his family that brought electricity and light to their home. As you read about William Kamkwamba, think about the qualities that made his achievements possible.

? THINK ABOUT IT

Who is someone you consider to be remarkable? What qualities do they have? How do you define remarkable?

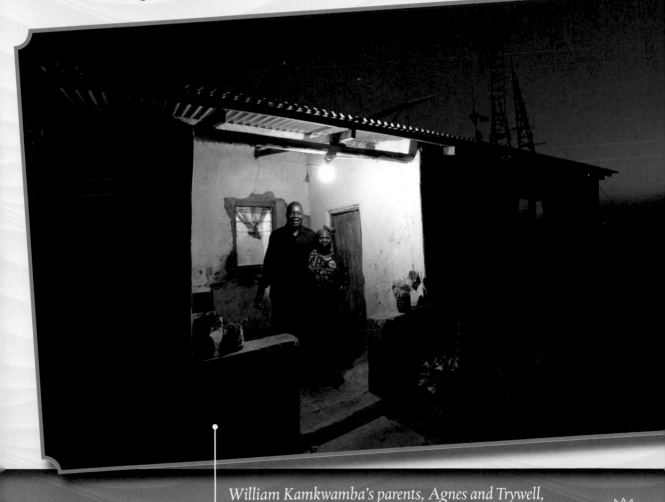

William Kamkwamba's parents, Agnes and Trywell, proudly stand in the brightly-lit entrance to their home.

At Home in Malawi

William Kamkwamba was born on August 5, 1987. He grew up in Malawi (mah-LAH-wee), a country in East Africa. There are more than 17 million people living there. It is sometimes called "the warm heart of Africa" for its kind-hearted people.

Wimbe Village

William is the second oldest child of Agnes and Trywell Kamkwamba. He has six sisters. There are ten homes in William's village of Wimbe (WIM-bay). Wimbe is just north of Malawi's capital city, Lilongwe. The people in Wimbe speak Chichewa (Chi-chey-wah), one of Malawi's official languages. Some also speak English.

The city of Lilongwe is the largest in Malawi with a population of 979,000.

No Rain...No Gain

In 2002, **drought** hit Malawi and caused **famine** in the country. William's family worked hard all year planting and growing maize, or white corn, but the drought destroyed it all. Eventually, the family's food was **rationed** to only one meal a day, which was a handful of *nsima* (en-See-ma)—a mixture of corn flour and water. Many people in Malawi starved to death during the famine.

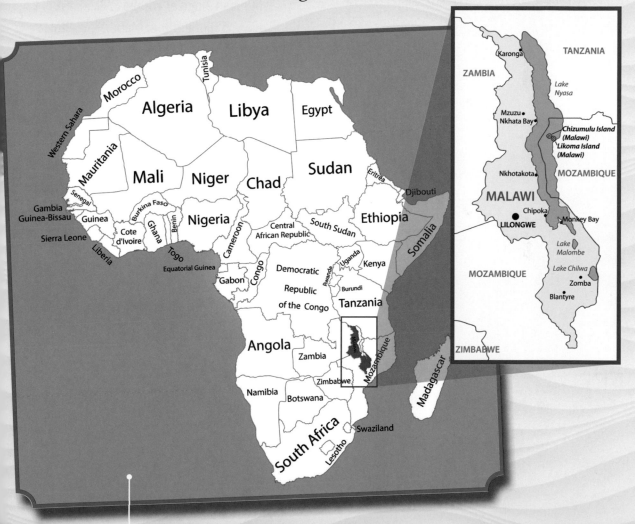

The country of Malawi is land-locked, meaning it does not border an ocean. Land-locked areas usually have less rain than areas on the water.

Dare to Dream

William's family's main source of income was from farming. When the drought happened, his family could no longer afford to pay for his education. William was determined to have a different life in the future, so he continued to learn even though he could not go to school. He visited his local library to read books about the subjects he had studied in school, including his favorite—science.

Drawing Power

One day, William found a book at the library about windmills. He discovered they could be used to create electricity. William studied the pictures and diagrams to learn how windmills were made.

The library in William's village received books donated from America, including the book on windmills titled Using Energy *by Mary D. Atwater.*

Hope for Change

In William's village, there was no electric light. William believed that if he could build his own windmill, he could create electricity using wind power. Electricity would make cooking easier. It would provide light after dark. With power from a windmill, people could use water from below the ground to **irrigate** crops and provide clean drinking water.

William and his sisters sometimes burned oil in lamps for light when studying at night. The smoke the lamps produced, however, often made them feel sick.

? THINK ABOUT IT

Imagine you were told you could no longer go to school. What would you do? The drought caused more than just hunger for William and his family. How did it force William to learn differently?

> " I'd never built anything like it before, but I knew if windmills existed on the cover of that book it meant another person had built them. After looking at it that way, I felt confident I could build one, too.
>
> —**William Kamkwamba,** *The Boy Who Harnessed the Wind*

It's Only Natural!

Renewable energy is energy that is made from natural resources. Renewable energy can be replaced, meaning that it will not run out. Resources such as water, sunlight, wind, and even animal waste provide renewable energy. This "clean energy" does not pollute the air or water.

Harnessed Wind

A windmill uses wind to create electricity. As wind blows, it moves the blades of the windmill. When the blades spin, they cause a **generator** to spin and create electricity.

blades   windmill

generator

This diagram shows how wind energy is used to create electricity.

From Trash to Treasure

William believed that his dream of creating electricity with wind energy would make life better for everyone in his village. He began searching for materials to build his invention, which he called "electric wind." He used many discarded items from other farmers, or things he found in the scrap yard, as parts for his windmill.

bicycle wheel

tractor fan

bamboo

William collected items such as a tractor fan, broken bicycle parts, and bamboo poles to construct his windmill.

Creativity in Motion

William didn't have the tools needed to build his windmill, so he used his creativity to make his own. He turned a piece of steel into a hammer. He made a drill by putting a nail through half a corn cob. In order to drill holes, William used heat from a fire to make the nail hot enough to poke through plastic.

? THINK ABOUT IT

How did creativity and imagination help William get everything he needed to construct his windmill? Find examples from the book to support your answer.

William's resourcefulness helped him turn everyday objects into tools for building his windmill.

The Mighty Dynamo

One thing William was missing for his windmill was a generator to create electricity. In Wimbe, people use lights on their bicycles to travel after dark. The lights are powered by a generator called a **Dynamo**. William wondered if a Dynamo would generate electricity for a windmill, too. When his friend Gilbert offered to pay for one, William finally had the missing piece for his wind machine.

dynamo

The movement of the front tire on this bicycle spins the Dynamo, which creates energy to light the bulb.

Garbage Collector

William's family didn't understand what he was trying to do. His sisters were angry that they had to work in the kitchen while William read books and collected junk. His mother worried about the garbage he collected. She thought William was going crazy. William's father wasn't sure about allowing his son to use their old broken bicycle parts to make a windmill, but in the end, he agreed. All of William's family watched to see if he could make his dream a reality.

? THINK ABOUT IT

Have you ever tried something that seemed impossible? Did people laugh at your ideas? Think about William Kamkwamba's creativity and perseverance. He never gave up on his idea.

William assembled his windmill on the ground, then attached it to the top of a tower made from tree branches.

Electric Wind

William achieved his goal of building a windmill in 2002. About 60 people came to see if his wind machine would work. Most of them laughed, but William just ignored them. Some even believed his machine somehow blew away storm clouds, which stopped rain from watering their crops. He proved them wrong!

Awesome Power

William wrapped wire around a light bulb. He hoped his windmill would create enough power to light the bulb. When he released the windmill blades, they began to spin. Everyone was shocked to see the light bulb glow!

People in the village were amazed to see William's windmill generate enough power to light a light bulb!

Charging Ahead

People in the community spread the word about William's invention. When the librarian came to see William's windmill, she finally understood his interest in energy and electricity. A journalist from a Malawian newspaper arrived to photograph the windmill and interview William about his remarkable machine.

> *People often ask me, "So how did you manage such a thing?" Well, I designed and built my machine in much the same way many Africans are getting by these days: by taking simple, everyday materials and being creative.*
>
> **—William Kamkwamba's blog**
> **http://williamkamkwamba.typepad.com/**
> **williamkamkwamba/2009/09/**

After William created his first windmill, he went on to create more windmills to provide power to his home and to irrigate crops.

Water from Wind

William wanted to be sure that even if another drought happened, water was still available for farming. He created a windmill pump for irrigation to access water underneath the ground. The water was pumped through a **borehole**. William's community now had access to water at any time.

The Wind is Picking Up

One day, a man named Dr. Hartford Mchazime (mik-HAZ-a-mee), came to see William and his windmill. Dr. Mchazime was from the Head Office of the Malawi Teacher Training Activity (MTTA), the organization responsible for bringing the library to William's village. He was one of William's greatest supporters.

On Air

A journalist from Malawi's Radio One program interviewed William about his windmill. When the interview came on, William's family gathered around the radio. His sisters cheered when they heard his voice come through the speakers.

As William's story became known throughout Malawi, he received many invitations to speak about his incredible accomplishments.

Transforming Power

An American living in Malawi wrote about William on his **blog**, which was seen by many people around the world. One of them was the program director for a conference called TEDGlobal. The yearly event invites scientists, inventors, and other people with new and exciting ideas to come together. William was asked to speak about his windmill at the conference in 2007.

William on the World Stage

TED stands for Technology, Entertainment, and Design. When William arrived at the conference, he met a man named Tom Rielly, an American TED organizer. Tom introduced William to the Internet. William had seen big computers when he was at high school, but none were working at the time.

Bola Olabisi speaks about GWIIN, the Global Women Inventors and Innovators Network, at TEDGlobal.

Among Friends

Even though William was shy, he overcame his nerves and told his unique story on the TED stage. When he finished speaking, the audience showed how much they admired him by standing and clapping.

> ...the most amazing thing about TED wasn't the Internet, the gadgets, or even the breakfast buffets... it was the other Africans who stood onstage each day and shared their stories and vision of how to make our continent a better place for our people.
>
> **—William Kamkwamba,
> The Boy Who Harnessed the Wind**

At TEDGlobal 2007, Kenya's James Shikwati shares his ideas about the economy.

Persevering People

Many of William's classmates shared his love for making their communities better. Many had similar difficulties to overcome. William felt very inspired by his classmates. Even when classes became challenging for him, he persevered because he was surrounded by people in the same situation.

> My fellow students and I talk about creating a new kind of Africa, a place of leaders instead of victims, a home of innovation rather than charity.
>
> —**William Kamkwamba at the African Leadership Academy**

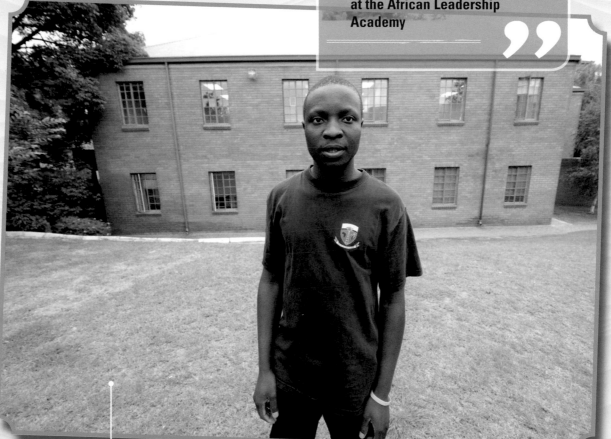

William was part of the Class of 2010, the first group to graduate from the African Leadership Academy in Johannesburg, South Africa.

Seeing is Believing

The connections and friendships William made at the TED conference led to many other opportunities, including a trip to America. William was invited to visit New York City, Los Angeles, and San Diego in December of 2007. He saw snow for the first time, went to the theater, visited museums, and ate a variety of foods.

William experienced the fast pace and large crowds in New York City. He even got to go to the top of the Empire State Building.

Western Exposure

William spent Christmas Day in Los Angeles, California. He went to the ocean and walked along the boardwalk. He even went to Disneyland! The highlight of his trip, however, was visiting a large **wind farm** in Palm Springs, California to see modern **turbines** in action. William was amazed by the size and number of the massive machines.

> *It was an incredible feeling to see the machines that I'd been imagining for so long. Now here they were, twisting in the wind before me. I'd come full circle.*
>
> **—William Kamkwamba,**
> **The Boy Who Harnessed the Wind**

William was amazed to see more than 6,000 wind turbines, each standing over 200 feet tall.

Telling His Story

William partnered with author Bryan Mealer in 2009 to write a book about his life called *The Boy Who Harnessed the Wind*. There is also a children's picture book version that was published in 2012. In 2013, he starred in a **documentary film** called *Moving Windmills*. William's story has been translated into many languages around the world.

William and his co-author, Bryan Mealer, were invited to appear on the television program, GOOD MORNING AMERICA in 2009 to speak about their book about William's story, called The Boy Who Harnessed the Wind.

Giving Back

William has also been able to make some simple changes for his family, such as buying new blankets, putting a new roof on their home, and buying his sisters real mattresses so they no longer slept on grass mats.

Paying It Forward

In 2010, William partnered with buildOn.org, a foundation that uses donated money to build schools. Together, they built a new primary school for 150 students in Wimbe. The school includes solid construction, bathrooms for boys and girls, classrooms, student laptops, electricity, fans, solar and wind power, and a large library. In the evenings, adult classes and community meetings are held at the school.

William installed solar panels at the local primary and high school to allow students to use donated computers. Solar panels trap the sun's energy to provide power.

Lighting the Way

William has been involved with many projects to bring health, education, and power to the people of Malawi. He purchased **malaria nets** for his community to keep mosquitoes from transmitting the virus to people while they sleep. He also wrote a play to bring awareness about **AIDS**, a disease that attacks the immune system.

Soccer Rules!

Other students were forced to drop out of school during the famine. William decided to create soccer teams, so children could spend their time playing soccer instead of getting into trouble. There were two teams—one for girls, and one for boys. The organization "Moving Windmills," which was inspired by William, provided the teams with uniforms and coaches. The games also provided an opportunity for women and families to make money selling food to people watching the games.

? THINK ABOUT IT

William Kamkwamba thought of others in his community, including the children. What would you do to bring change to your community?

Soccer, also known as football, is a popular sport played throughout Africa.

Writing Prompts

1. Think about the ways you are similar to William, and how you may be different. Imagine that you traded places for a year. How would your life change? How would it remain the same?

2. William Kamkwamba's story is full of hope, creativity, and perseverance. What are some of your own character qualities that will help you achieve your dreams? Consider starting a diary or journal, and record your thoughts, ideas, and experiences every day. Everyone has a unique story to tell!

Learning More

Books

The Boy Who Harnessed the Wind. Kamkwamba, William and Bryan Mealer. William Morrow/Harper Collins Publishing Company, 2009.

Energy Revolution: Generating Wind Power. Walker, Niki. Crabtree Publishing Company, 2007.

Understanding Wind Power. Goodman, Polly. Gareth Stevens Publishing, 2011.

Websites

www.williamkamkwamba.typepad.com/
William's blog. Read more about his inspiring experiences.

www.movingwindmills.org/
This is an organization that raises money to help support the people of Malawi as they develop their economy, education, and health.

www.kidwind.org
Learn how to build your own windmill and discover more about renewable energy.

www.eia.gov/kids/energy.cfm?page=about_forms_of_energy-basics
A website about energy by the U.S. Energy Information Administration. Discover where energy comes from, the different forms of energy, and how it can be used in our daily lives.

www.buildon.org/
buildOn.org brings communities together to build new schools in some of the poorest areas of the world so every child has the opportunity to receive an education.

Glossary

AIDS (Acquired Immunodeficiency Syndrome) A disease which attacks a person's cells and can cause their immune system to fail

blog A website or webpage that expresses personal opinions

borehole A vertical or horizontal hole drilled deep into the ground.

documentary film A movie that is a true story about something or someone

drought A long period of dry weather that harms crops

Dynamo A generator built into the front wheel of a bicycle that powers a light bulb

famine A shortage of food usually caused by a drought

generator A machine that changes the type of energy used for power

irrigate To water plants or crops with water taken from a source such as underground

malaria A common virus carried by mosquitoes that causes high fever, dizziness, and sometimes, death

rationed Controlling the amount of something, such as food

recycle To use something someone no longer wants for a new purpose

sustainability The ability to use something without completely destroying or wasting it

turbines Spinning blades that are powered by air, water, or gas to produce electricity

wind farm Land on which turbines or windmills are built to generate electricity

Index